Some people think I'm just a pet.
They haven't gotten to know me yet.

I'm a reliable friend and a comfort, too.
Sometimes you'll think I'm just like you.

This is our scrapbook we can share.
It shows how much you really care.

I know you'll like it and you'll see.
We share a lot of fond memories.

Gather those pictures of cute things I do.
Be as proud of me as I am of you.

Created by Susan and Kerry Kelley,
with contributions by Erin and Lindsay Kelley

Susan Kelley Pet Diaries
Richmond, Virginia
www.petphotodiary.com
ISBN 0-9771624-0-0

My Puppy Picture

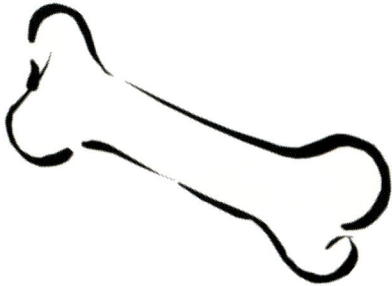

Hi there!

My name is _____

This book is all about me!!

My Baby Picture

My hair color is _____

My eyes are _____

I am a _____ boy _____ girl

I am

_____ a registered purebred

_____ simply a proud mix

My birthday is

_____

I was born here

_____

Snapshots

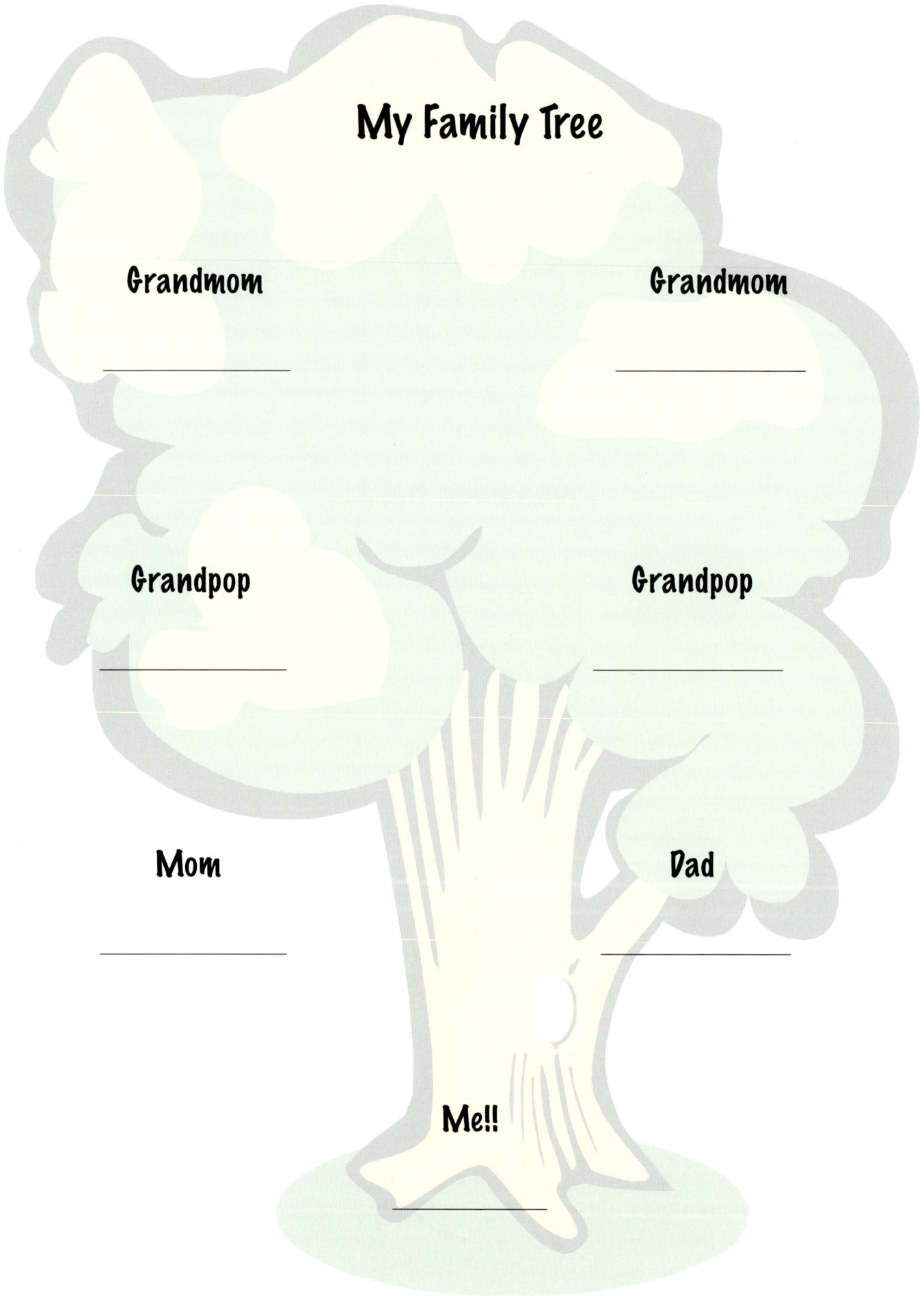

My Family Tree

Grandmom

_____

Grandmom

_____

Grandpop

_____

Grandpop

_____

Mom

_____

Dad

_____

Me!!

_____

I was a cuddly puppy.

Snapshots

More cuddly pictures...

Snapshots

My visits to the vet.

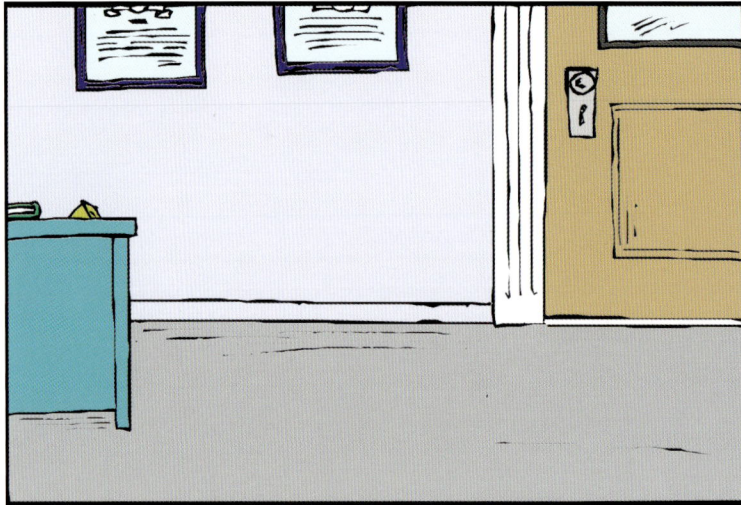

Vet's name: _____

Address: _____

Phone: _____

Fears I may have: _____

Well, nobody likes shots!

Medical records

visit _____

reason _____

visit _____

reason _____

visit _____

reason _____

visit _____

reason _____

visit _____

reason _____

Did I need any surgeries?

Better make some notes...

Was I a good patient?

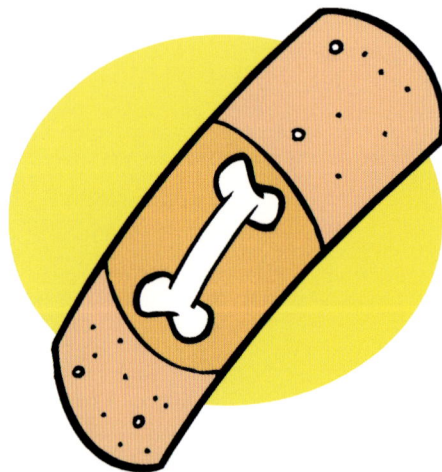

or did I only mope?

This is my proud new family

Snapshots

and cute pictures they took of me.

Snapshots

These are some things I like to do

Snapshots

Sometimes alone

Sometimes with you

These are my friends who like to play.

Snapshots

Some live close, some far away.

Snapshots

These are the things I love to eat...

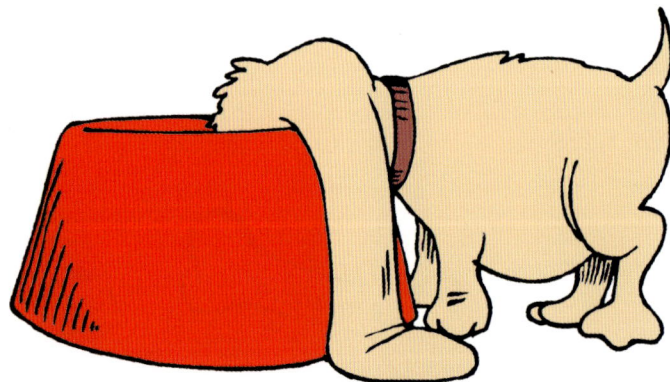

These are the tricks I do for treats...

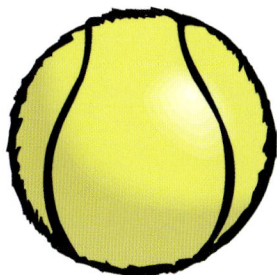

There are many good reasons I need to bark,

DELIVERY

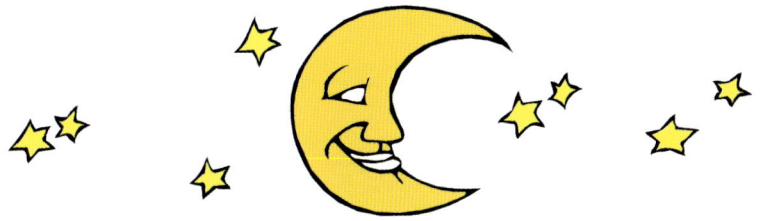

Sometimes it's daylight, sometimes it's dark!

Here are a few places I like to be.

These are some of my best memories!

There are so many pictures as you can see!

Snapshots

My friends, family and just precious me!

Thanks for loving me!